PIANO • VOCAL • GUITAR

THE BEST OF
HANK WILLIAMS

Hal Leonard Publishing Corporation

7777 West Bluemound Road P.O. Box 13819 Milwaukee, WI 53213

ISBN 0-7935-0087-7

ALABAMA WALTZ

Words and Music by
HANK WILLIAMS

Gracefully

mf

C   F

I was sad and blue,___ I was down - heart - ed too___ It

C   G7   C

seemed like the whole world was lost___ Then I took a

F   C   G7

chance___ and we hap-pened___ to dance To the tune of The Al - a-bam-a

Ped.

BABY, WE'RE REALLY IN LOVE

Words and Music by
HANK WILLIAMS

THE BLUES COME AROUND

Words and Music by
HANK WILLIAMS

CHORUS

Oh, THE BLUES COME A-ROUND_____ Yes, THE BLUES COME A - ROUND_____

_____ Lawd, THE BLUES COME A-ROUND ev - 'ry eve - 'nin' when the sun_____ goes

1. down._____ 2. down._____

3

I built my castles very high
And then she went and said goodbye
And ever since she tore 'em down
The blues come around when the sun
    goes down.

4

Once she called me all her own
But now she's gone and I'm alone
And ev'ry evenin' I'm sorrow bound
'Cause the blues come around when
    the sun goes down.

CALLING YOU

Words and Music by
HANK WILLIAMS

1. When you've strayed from the fold and there's trou-ble in your
2. (As you) jour-ney day by day and temp-ta-tion comes your
3. (When your) soul is bur-dened down and your friends can-not be

soul. Can't you hear the bles-sed Sav-iour CALL-ING YOU?
way. Can't you hear the bles-sed Sav-iour CALL-ING YOU?
found. Can't you hear the bles-sed Sav-iour CALL-ING YOU?

When your soul is lost in sin and you're at your jour-ney's
If you fol-low 'in His light He will al-ways guide you
If you'll fol-low Him each day He will bright-en up your

COLD, COLD HEART

Words and Music by
HANK WILLIAMS

COUNTRYFIED

Brightly

Words and Music by
HANK WILLIAMS

DEAR BROTHER

Words and Music by
HANK WILLIAMS

EVERYTHING'S OKAY

Words and Music by
HANK WILLIAMS

The hogs took the cholera and they've all done died, the bees got mad and they left the hive. The weevils got the
The well's gone dry and I have to tote the water, up from the spring about a mile and a quarter. My helper, he quit

corn and the rain rotted the hay, but we're still a-livin' so EVERYTHING'S OKAY. The porch rotted down, that's more
for lack of pay, but we're still a-livin' so EVERYTHING'S OKAY. The house, it leaks, it needs a new top, when it rains

expense, the durned old mule, he tore down the fence. The mortgage is due and I can't pay
it wets everything   we got. The chimney fell down just the other day   but we're still a-livin'

so EVERYTHING'S OKAY but we're still a-livin' so EVERYTHING'S OKAY.

3

The corn meal's gone and the meat's run out, got nothing to kill to put in the smokehouse
The preacher's coming Sunday to spend the day, but we're still a-livin' so EVERYTHING'S OKAY
The canned stuff's spoiled or else the jars got broke, and all we got left is one old Billy goat
We're gonna have a new baby about the first of May, but we're still a-livin' so EVERYTHING'S OKAY
My crop, it rotted in the ground, I asked for another loan but the banker turned me down
But we're still a-livin' and we're prayin' for better days, so after all everything's in pretty good shape

HELP ME UNDERSTAND

Words and Music by
HANK WILLIAMS

Quietly

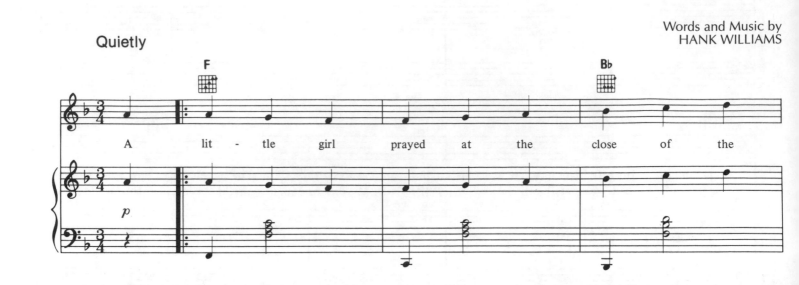

A lit - tle girl prayed at the close of the

day____ 'Cause her dad - dy had gone far a -

way. On her lit - tle face was a look of des -

take me and lead me and hold to my

hand_____ Oh, Heav - en - ly Fath - er, Help

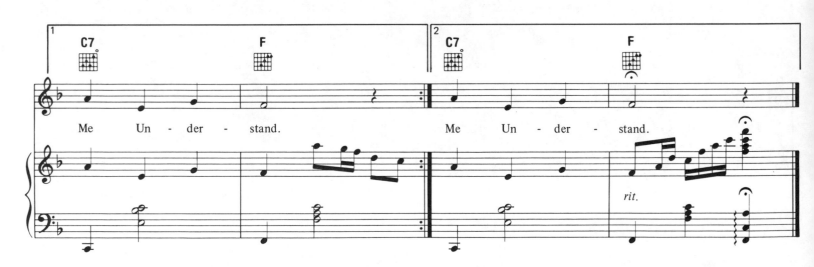

Me Un - der - stand. Me Un - der - stand.

rit.

RECITATION

You know, Friends, I wonder how many homes are broken tonight - just how many tears are shed.
    By some little word of anger that never should have been said
I'd like to tell you a story of a family I once knew
    We'll call them Mary and William and their little daughter, Sue
Mary was just a plain Mother, and Bill - well, he was the usual Dad
    And they had their family quarrels, like everyone else - but neither one got mad
Then one day something happened - it was nothing, of course
    But one word led to another, and the last word led to a divorce.
Now here were two grown up people who failed to see common sense
    They strengthened their own selfish pride - at little Sue's expense
You know, she didn't ask to be brought into this world - to drift from pillar to post
    But a divorce never stops to consider the one it hurts the most
There'd be a lot more honest lovin' in this wicked world today
    If just a few parted parents could hear little Sue say:

(Repeat Chorus)

HEY, GOOD LOOKIN'

Words and Music by
HANK WILLIAMS

HONKY TONK BLUES

Moderately Slow

Words and Music by
HANK WILLIAMS

HONKY TONKIN'

Words and Music by
HANK WILLIAMS

Moderately

A HOUSE WITHOUT LOVE

Words and Music by
HANK WILLIAMS

HOW CAN YOU REFUSE HIM NOW

Words and Music by
HANK WILLIAMS

I AIN'T GOT NOTHING BUT TIME

Words and Music by
HANK WILLIAMS

CHORUS

Well, I AIN'T GOT NOTH-ING BUT TIME _____ So, Ba-by, if you want to

shine _____ If you'll take time to look, my num-ber's in the book And

you can call me an-y time. _____ 2. I'm time. _____

3. If you

4

No use to sit at home and pine
And let someone trouble your mind
Just come along with me
There's more fish in the sea
And I AIN'T GOT NOTHING BUT TIME

5

Now, Baby, just come on and smile
You'll find that life is still worthwhile
If you'll just look around
There's lots of fellows in this town
That for you ain't got nothing but time

I CAN'T GET YOU OFF OF MY MIND

Words and Music by
HANK WILLIAMS

I CAN'T HELP IT
(IF I'M STILL IN LOVE WITH YOU)

Words and Music by
HANK WILLIAMS

Mournfully

I SAW THE LIGHT

Words and Music by
HANK WILLIAMS

45

I WISH YOU DIDN'T LOVE ME SO MUCH

Words and Music by
HANK WILLIAMS

INTRO.

CHORUS

1. Well, you say___ "Get out and you bet-ter stay gone" then you
2. (Now the) preach-er man said, "For___ bet-ter or worse"

have a big po-lice-man___ drag me back home You tell him good and loud "Put him
Late-ly I've been look-in' for that big___ black hearse I wish___ to my soul you'd___

in the cal-a-boose," then you cry and ask the judge___ to___
slow___ down the pace 'cause I tell you right___ now the hide's___

I'LL NEVER GET OUT
OF THIS WORLD ALIVE

Words by FRED ROSE
Music by HANK WILLIAMS

Moderately

Now you're look-in' at a man that's get-tin' kind-a mad___ I've had a lot of luck but it's
buy a Sun-day suit and it would leave me broke___ If it had two pair of pants I would

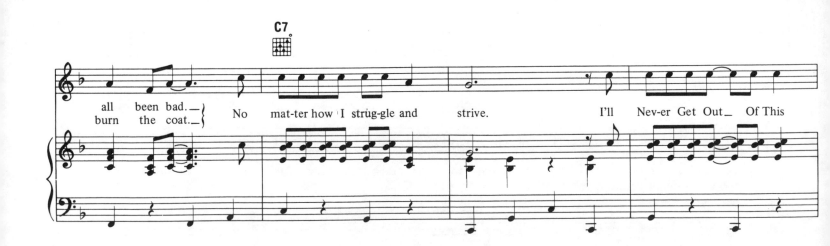

all been bad.___ No mat-ter how I strug-gle and strive. I'll Nev-er Get Out___ Of This
burn the coat.___

52

JAMBALAYA (ON THE BAYOU)

Words and Music by
HANK WILLIAMS

Moderately

see my ma cher a - mi - o_____ Pick guitar, fill fruit jar and be gay - o_____ Son of a
gun, we'll have big fun on the bay - ou_____
Thi - bo - bay - ou_____

rit.   mp

3. Settle down far from town, get me a pirogue
   And I'll catch all the fish in the bayou
   Swap my mon to buy Yvonne what whe need-o
   Son of a gun, we'll have big fun on the bayou

I'M A LONG GONE DADDY

Words and Music by
HANK WILLIAMS

I'M SO LONESOME I COULD CRY

Words and Music by
HANK WILLIAMS

KAW-LIGA

Words by FRED ROSE
Music by HANK WILLIAMS

Insistently

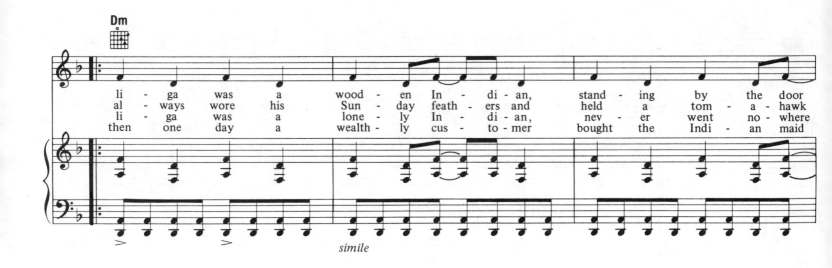

li - ga was a wood - en In - di - an, stand - ing by the door
al - ways wore his Sun - day feath - ers and held a tom - a - hawk
then one day a wealth - ly cus - to - mer bought the Indi - an maid

simile

He fell in love with an In - di - an maid - en
The maid - en wore her beads and braids and
His heart was set on the In - di - an maid - en
And took her, oh, so far a - way but

THE LITTLE HOUSE WE BUILT

Words and Music by
HANK WILLIAMS

LONG GONE LONESOME BLUES

Words and Music by
HANK WILLIAMS

I went down to the riv-er to watch the fish swim by.
find me a riv-er One that's cold as ice.

But I got to the riv-er so lone-some I want-ed to die. Oh,
When I find me that riv-er Lawd I'm gon-na pay the price Oh,

Lawd And then I jumped in the riv-er but the dog-gone riv-er was dry. I
Lawd I'm go-in' down in it three times but I'm on-ly com-in' up twice. She

A MANSION ON THE HILL

Words by FRED ROSE
Music by HANK WILLIAMS

Moderately

To -

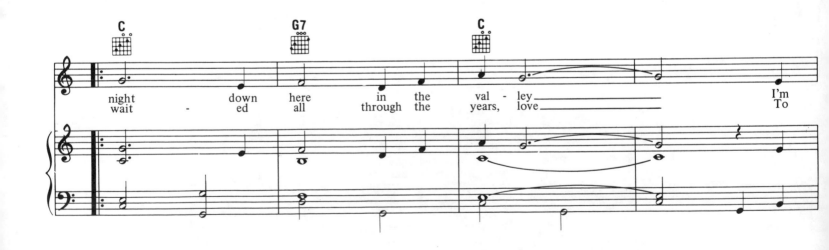

night down here in the val - ley I'm
wait - ed all through the years, love To

MOANIN' THE BLUES

Words and Music by
HANK WILLIAMS

MIND YOUR OWN BUSINESS

Words and Music by
HANK WILLIAMS

3. I might tell a lot of stories that may not be true
   But I can get to heaven just as easy as you
   Why don't you Mind Your Own Bus'ness, Mind Your Own Bus'ness
   Well, if you mind your bus'ness then you won't be mindin' mine
   Mindin' other peoples' bus'ness seems to be high-tone
   But I got all that I can do just mindin' my own
   Why don't you Mind Your Own Bus'ness, Mind Your Own Bus'ness
   Well if you mind your bus'ness you'll stay busy all the time.

MOVE IT ON OVER

Words and Music by
HANK WILLIAMS

MY SON CALLS ANOTHER MAN DADDY

Words by JEWELL HOUSE
Music by HANK WILLIAMS

RAMBLIN' MAN

Words and Music by
HANK WILLIAMS

Moderately Slow

THERE'S A TEAR IN MY BEER

Words and Music by
HANK WILLIAMS

83

THERE'LL BE NO TEARDROPS TONIGHT

Words and Music by
HANK WILLIAMS

Moderately

tend_____ I'm free from sor - row ____ Make be -
lieve _____ that you still love me ____ When you

YOU WIN AGAIN

Words and Music by
HANK WILLIAMS

WHY DON'T YOU LOVE ME

Words and Music by
HANK WILLIAMS

YOU'RE GONNA CHANGE
(OR I'M GONNA LEAVE)

Words and Music by
HANK WILLIAMS

YOUR CHEATIN' HEART

Words and Music by
HANK WILLIAMS

96